Bb TRUMPET 2

PERFORMANCE FAVORITES

Volume 1

Band Arrangements Correlated with
Essential Elements® Band Method Book 2

Page	Title	Composer/Arranger	Correlated with Essential Elements Book 2 Page
3	African Sketches	James Curnow	15
4	Barrier Reef	John Higgins	15
5	Do You Hear What I Hear	arr. Michael Sweeney	15
6	Regimental Honor	John Moss	15
7	Spinning Wheel	arr. Michael Sweeney	15
8	Streets of Madrid	John Moss	15
9	You're A Grand Old Flag	arr. Paul Lavender	15
10	British Masters Suite	arr. John Moss	32
12	Elves' Dance	arr. Paul Lavender	32
13	Firebird Suite – Finale	arr. John Moss	32
14	Gaelic Dances	John Moss	32
16	Irish Legends	James Curnow	32
17	On Broadway	arr. Michael Sweeney	32
18	Summon the Heroes	arr. Michael Sweeney	32
19	Two Celtic Folksongs	arr. Paul Lavender	32

ISBN 978-1-4234-5782-4

HAL•LEONARD®

7777 W. BLUEMOUND RD. P.O. BOX 13819 MILWAUKEE, WI 53213

00860194

AFRICAN SKETCHES
(Based on African Folk Songs)

Bb TRUMPET 2

JAMES CURNOW (ASCAP)

00860194

BARRIER REEF
Overture For Band

Bb TRUMPET 2

JOHN HIGGINS (ASCAP

DO YOU HEAR WHAT I HEAR

Words and Music by
NOEL REGNEY and GLORIA SHAYNE
Arranged by MICHAEL SWEENEY

B♭ TRUMPET 2

00860194

REGIMENTAL HONOR

Bb TRUMPET 2

JOHN MOSS (ASCAP)

Recorded by BLOOD, SWEAT, & TEARS
SPINNING WHEEL

**Words and Music by
DAVID CLAYTON THOMAS**
Arranged by MICHAEL SWEENEY

Bb TRUMPET 2

THE STREETS OF MADRID

Bb TRUMPET 2

JOHN MOSS

00860194

YOU'RE A GRAND OLD FLAG

Bb TRUMPET 2

Words and Music by GEORGE M. COHAN
Arranged by PAUL LAVENDER

00860194

BRITISH MASTERS SUITE

Bb TRUMPET 2

Arranged by JOHN MOSS

I. Marching Song

GUSTAV HOLST

II. Nimrod (From "Enigma Variations")

EDWARD ELGAR

molto rit.

III. Sine Nomine

RALPH VAUGHAN WILLIAMS

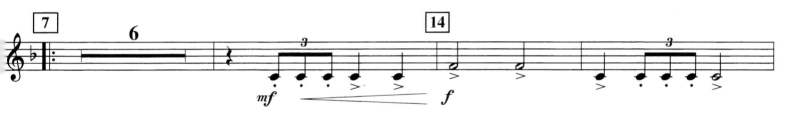

ELVES' DANCE
(From The Nutcracker)

Bb TRUMPET 2

PETER I. TCHAIKOVSKY
Arranged by PAUL LAVENDER

FIREBIRD SUITE – Finale

B♭ TRUMPET 2

IGOR STRAVINSKY
Arranged by JOHN MOSS

GAELIC DANCES

Bb TRUMPET 2

Arranged by JOHN MOS

IRISH LEGENDS

Bb TRUMPET 2

JAMES CURNOW (ASCAP)

ON BROADWAY

**Words and Music by BARRY MANN, CYNTHIA WEIL,
MIKE STOLLER and JERRY LEIBER**
Arranged by MICHAEL SWEENEY

B♭ TRUMPET 2

Written for the 100th Anniversary Celebration of the Modern Olympic Games

SUMMON THE HEROES

(For Tim Morrison)

Bb TRUMPET 2

By JOHN WILLIAM
Arranged by MICHAEL SWEENI

00862120

00860194

TWO CELTIC FOLKSONGS

(The Maids of Mourne Shore • The Star of the County Down)

Celtic Folksongs
Arranged by PAUL LAVENDER

TRUMPET 2

"The Maids of Mourne Shore"

Dolce

Slightly Faster

Tempo I

With Energy

"The Star of the County Down"

Slowly

A Tempo

860194